J 910
Oachs
Arcti

$22.95
ocn921821724

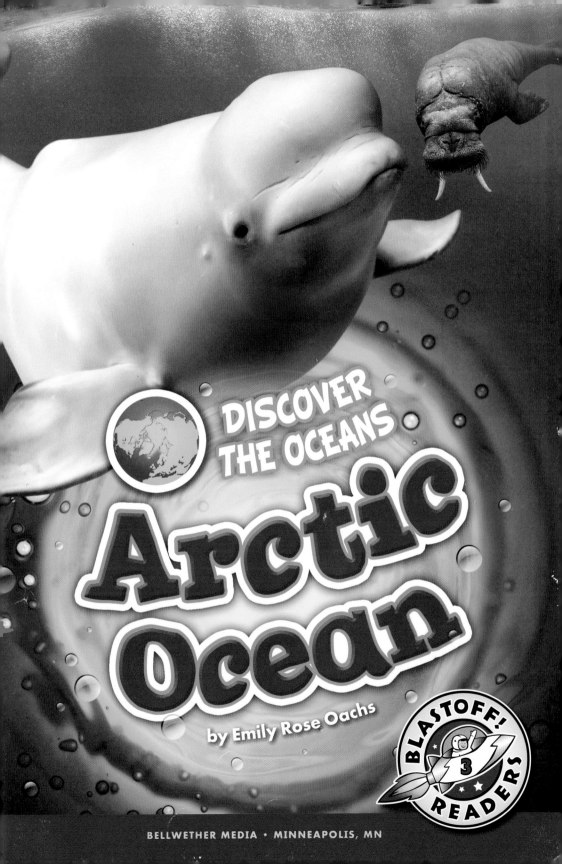

DISCOVER THE OCEANS

Arctic Ocean

by Emily Rose Oachs

BLASTOFF!
3
READERS

BELLWETHER MEDIA · MINNEAPOLIS, MN

Note to Librarians, Teachers, and Parents:

Blastoff! Readers are carefully developed by literacy experts and combine standards-based content with developmentally appropriate text.

Level 1 provides the most support through repetition of high-frequency words, light text, predictable sentence patterns, and strong visual support.

Level 2 offers early readers a bit more challenge through varied simple sentences, increased text load, and less repetition of high-frequency words.

Level 3 advances early-fluent readers toward fluency through increased text and concept load, less reliance on visuals, longer sentences, and more literary language.

Level 4 builds reading stamina by providing more text per page, increased use of punctuation, greater variation in sentence patterns, and increasingly challenging vocabulary.

Level 5 encourages children to move from "learning to read" to "reading to learn" by providing even more text, varied writing styles, and less familiar topics.

Whichever book is right for your reader, Blastoff! Readers are the perfect books to build confidence and encourage a love of reading that will last a lifetime!

This edition first published in 2016 by Bellwether Media, Inc.

No part of this publication may be reproduced in whole or in part without written permission of the publisher. For information regarding permission, write to Bellwether Media, Inc., Attention: Permissions Department, 5357 Penn Avenue South, Minneapolis, MN 55419.

Library of Congress Cataloging-in-Publication Data

Oachs, Emily Rose.
  Arctic Ocean / by Emily Rose Oachs.
    pages cm. – (Blastoff! Readers: Discover the Oceans)
  Summary: "Simple text and full-color photography introduce beginning readers to the Arctic Ocean. Developed by literacy experts for students in kindergarten through third grade"–Provided by publisher.
  Audience: Ages 5-8.
  Audience: K to grade 3.
  Includes bibliographical references and index.
  ISBN 978-1-62617-330-9 (hardcover : alk. paper)
  1. Arctic Ocean–Juvenile literature. I. Title.
  GC401.O24 2016
  910.9163'2-dc23
                              2015029352

Printed in the United States of America, North Mankato, MN.

Table of Contents

The Smallest Ocean

The Arctic is the smallest and coldest of the five oceans. It covers 5.4 million square miles (14 million square kilometers).

The Arctic Ocean sits at the top of the world. Its icy waters surround the **North Pole**.

DID YOU KNOW?

- Explorers Frederick Cook and Robert Peary both claimed to have reached the North Pole first. However, neither actually made it.

- The North Pole spends six months in darkness and six months in sunlight each year.

- In some places, Arctic ice may drift several miles per day from wind and currents.

lion's mane jellyfish

- Lion's mane jellyfish live in the Arctic Ocean. They may grow to be 100 feet (30 meters) long!

Where Is the Arctic Ocean?

The Arctic Ocean lies in the Northern, Eastern, and Western **hemispheres**. Its waters flow into the Chukchi, Barents, Kara, and other seas.

Asia, Europe, North America, and Greenland surround the Arctic. The ocean forms their northern borders.

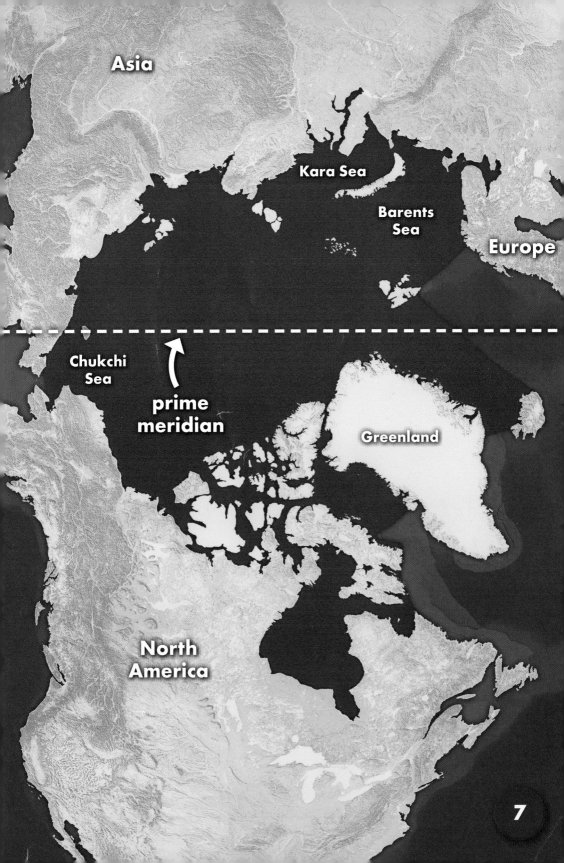

Asia

Kara Sea

Barents
Sea

Europe

Chukchi
Sea

prime
meridian

Greenland

North
America

7

Water at the Arctic's surface is ice cold. In winter, its temperature drops to **freezing**, or 28 degrees Fahrenheit (-2 degrees Celsius). Deeper water is slightly warmer.

8

iceberg

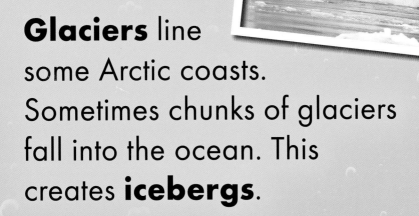
glacier

Glaciers line some Arctic coasts. Sometimes chunks of glaciers fall into the ocean. This creates **icebergs**.

Wide **basins** stretch beneath
Arctic waters. Underwater
mountain chains rise beside them.
Hidden below the ocean floor
are oil and natural gas.

Currents push water in and out of the Arctic Ocean. Fishers cast nets where warmer currents meet chilly ocean waters.

The Polar Ice Pack

A thick layer of floating ice regularly covers much of the Arctic Ocean. This is the **polar ice pack**. It can be more than 15 feet (5 meters) thick!

The summer sun melts parts of the pack. Winter adds ice again.

polar ice
pack

Recently, the ice pack has been getting smaller. **Global warming** keeps the melted ice from refreezing.

A disappearing ice pack changes the Arctic **climate**. It affects the homes of many animals.

The Plants and Animals

Arctic seaweed grows on the ocean floor. Near the surface, **phytoplankton** float in groups. These tiny plants are food for many ocean animals.

phytoplankton

Few other plants
live in the Arctic Ocean. Little
sunlight and cold temperatures
keep plants from growing.

The Arctic Ocean is home to many **mammals**. Walruses, seals, narwhals, and whales swim below the surface.

harp seal

narwhal

walrus

beluga whale

polar bears

Polar bears roam the ice pack. They need it to survive. The icy Arctic is a **fragile** home.

Fast Facts About the Arctic Ocean

Size: 5.4 million square miles (14 million square kilometers); smallest ocean

Average Depth: 3,238 feet (987 meters)

Greatest Depth: 18,051 feet (5,502 meters)

Major Bodies of Water: Greenland Sea, Barents Sea, Kara Sea, Laptev Sea, East Siberian Sea, Chukchi Sea, Beaufort Sea, Hudson Bay, Baffin Bay

Continents Touched: North America, Europe, Asia

Total Coastline: 28,203 miles (45,389 kilometers)

Top Natural Resources: oil, natural gas, fish, seals, whales

HMS *Erebus*

Famous Shipwrecks:
- HMS *Fury* (1825)
- HMS *Erebus* (1846)
- HMS *Terror* (1846)
- HMS *Achates* (1942)

Asia

Kara Sea

Laptev
Sea

Barents Sea

East
Siberian
Sea

Europe

Arctic Ocean

Chukchi
Sea

Greenland
Sea

Beaufort
Sea

Baffin
Bay

North
America

Hudson
Bay

Glossary

basins—large areas of lower land in the ocean floor

climate—the weather patterns in an area over a long period of time

currents—large patterns of water movement in an ocean

fragile—easily broken or destroyed

freezing—the temperature at which water freezes into ice; salt water freezes at about 28 degrees Fahrenheit (-2 degrees Celsius).

glaciers—massive sheets of ice that cover large areas of land

global warming—the increase in temperature in Earth's atmosphere; scientists believe global warming is caused in part by human activity.

hemispheres—halves of the globe; the equator and prime meridian divide Earth into different hemispheres.

icebergs—large chunks of floating ice that have broken off from a glacier

mammals—warm-blooded animals that have backbones and feed their young milk

North Pole—the northernmost spot on Earth

phytoplankton—tiny ocean plants that drift

polar ice pack—the thick layer of frozen seawater that covers the Arctic Ocean

To Learn More

AT THE LIBRARY
Crawford, Laura. *In Arctic Waters*. Mount Pleasant, S.C.: Sylvan Dell Pub, 2007.

Simon, Seymour. *Global Warming*. New York, N.Y.: HarperCollins, 2010.

Spilsbury, Louise and Richard. *Arctic Ocean*. Chicago, Ill.: Heinemann Library, 2015.

ON THE WEB
Learning more about the Arctic Ocean is as easy as 1, 2, 3.

1. Go to www.factsurfer.com.

2. Enter "Arctic Ocean" into the search box.

3. Click the "Surf" button and you will see a list of related web sites.

With factsurfer.com, finding more information is just a click away.

Index